Amelia Saint George's

painted
furniture
and walls

Amelia Saint George's
painted furniture
and walls

HarperCollins*Publishers*

My thanks to the following tutors who have given me invaluable advice: Trisha Austin (Fine Art), Steve Alley (Sculpture), Tim Beswick (Sculpture). A very special thank you to Simon Betts who introduced me to playing with acrylic paint and is a fabulous teacher. Also to Maria Donato (Ceramics), Jill Raven (Textiles), Jo Miller (Sculpture), Gillian O'Bryon (Textiles), Dido Powell (Visual Studies) and to my artist friends Andrew Fergusson-Cuninghame, Richard Foster and last but not least, for his continual encouragement and advice, Anthony Greville-Bell.

My thanks to two-year-old Eleanor Michotte for her helpful hand prints over the toy boxes, and to her mother Letitia for bringing her over.

First published in 1996 by HarperCollins Publishers, London

A catalogue record for this book is available from the British Library

ISBN 0 00 412996 2

Edited by Geraldine Christy
Designed by Town Group Consultancy Ltd
Photography by John Freeman

Set in Pertus and Quay

Colour origination by Colourscan, Singapore
Printed and bound by Rotolito Lombada, Milan, Italy

Contents

Introduction

Today's new acrylic paints make applying decoration to furniture and walls not only possible but easy. Acrylics dry quickly, and they are odourless and economical. You can wipe away marks with water and wash your brushes in water, as long as you do so immediately after use.

I had little confidence in my own freehand painting and had always stuck to stencilling. However, the problem of how to paint directly onto my own furniture intrigued me, so I worked out a foolproof method of using a template to help me as I worked. Having decided where to place my motif, I traced through as many of the lines as I needed and then almost painted by numbers. Even as my confidence grew I glanced at the template for guidance on shading.

There are eight sheets of templates at the back of the book for you to cut out and use immediately by tracing. The designs vary from roses, rose hips and ribbon to tumbling lemon fruits and flowers, from small dots and leaves to trailing ivy, and from a meandering daisy chain to the three-dimensional effects of simple *trompe l'œil* flowers entwined in plasterwork. Whether you choose to enlarge or reduce the templates the method is the same.

Throughout the book there are assorted projects, ranging from a small box or tray to larger bookshelves and bedroom furniture. As well as transforming furniture you can also create attractive wall decoration rather than buying expensive wallpapers. New acrylic wall paints are also available and are pleasant to use.

All the techniques used in the book – rough and soft stippling, wood graining, sponging, dragging, colourwashing and stencilling – are all explained so that you have every technique and trick used at your fingertips. The book begins very simply and progresses through a variety of decorating ideas, from a child's room to an outside metal table, from soft pastel colours to bright, dynamic ones.

There are so many choices available to you when you decorate your furniture and walls just as you wish – no limitations of colour, size or proportion. You can paint anything – so do have a go!

7

Materials and techniques

COLOURS

I use artists' acrylic paints, which dry quickly, have no odour and are water washable.

I only use six primary colours:

Lemon Yellow – just the colour of a lemon with a hint of blue.
Cadmium Yellow – a stronger yellow with a hint of red in it.
Cadmium Red – a strong basic red with a warm yellow hidden in it.
Crimson – a deep red with a tendency towards blue.
Ultramarine – a wonderful deep blue with the warmth and depth of red within.
Coeruleum – a duller blue with a tendency to yellow.

When you place these colours in a circle you will have two yellows, two reds and two blues, giving you the ability to mix a range of colours with ease. By mixing colours related to each other you can achieve clearer colours. I have explained this more fully on page 24 and the chapter on 'Colour and the palette' presents attractive projects that will enable you to try out your colour skills.

If you follow the principle of mixing colours that are in harmony with each other as you work around the colour circle you will find, first the great joy of not only making your own colours, but also that of being able to re-mix them identically when you want to. Also, it is much less expensive to only use six colours. Black and white I normally use away from my main palette.

PALETTES

In my opinion the best way to use acrylics is with a Stay-Wet Palette. Acrylics dry quickly but this palette keeps them wet from underneath. Even when my acrylics are squeezed onto a china plate I keep a mist water-sprayer to hand, and cover the plate when not in use with film food wrap.

BRUSHES

Dalon artists' brushes are exceptionally versatile. Series D77 are round and tapered, come in all sizes and have good pointing characteristics. Series D88 are square edged and ideal for laying down larger areas of paint. Series D99 'Rigger' brushes are fine, with long, tapered hair. They are useful for painting lines and lettering.

Always use a good quality soft varnish brush and hide it away when not in use. It is all too easy to wreck beautiful work with a clumsy varnish brush.

SPECIALIST TOOLS FOR PAINT EFFECTS

You will need a number of specialist items for creating paint effects on walls.

To apply paint to the wall use a tray and roller. A chamois leather is used for rag rolling, a plastic stippling tool for a rough stippled effect, and a sponge for a soft sponged pattern. Use a stippling brush for softer stippling, a long-bristled brush for dragging, a wide-bristled brush for applying a colourwash and a plastic roller for wood graining.

Previous page *Six colours form my basic palette and with a few good quality brushes I am ready to paint.*

Right *Tools for paint effects. In clockwise direction: chamois leather strips tied into a bundle, tray and roller, rough plastic stippling brush, natural sponge, soft bristle stippling brush, long bristle dragging brush, plastic wood-grain roller and wide colourwash brush.*

STIPPLING

Apply the paint, then stipple it off with a soft dabbing motion. Occasionally 'empty' your brush by dabbing it onto kitchen paper.

RAG ROLLING

Apply the paint, then roll the chamois leather over the paint in a tumbling motion.

DRAGGING

Apply the paint, then drag it off with long downward brush strokes using a dragging brush. You will need to practice if you are tackling larger areas of paint that involve dashing up and down ladders.

ROUGH STIPPLING

Apply the paint, then stamp down the special tool. You can also swirl the tool or drag it to create lines; it is more versatile than may at first appear.

WOOD GRAINING

Apply the paint, then just drag the wood-graining roller through the paint, gently rocking it back and forth. This produces a wonderful effect of wood graining very simply.

STENCILLING

Take a piece of stencil card and cut out your motif. Using very little paint on a short squat stencil brush, apply the paint with a short tapping motion.

SPONGING

Gently apply a little paint to a natural sponge. Test it on kitchen paper for splodges, then gently apply the paint to the wall using a short tapping motion, applying more pressure to the sponge as the paint runs out. Combining colours gives subtle effects.

COLOURWASHING

With a sparing application of paint on your brush apply swift criss-cross strokes of colour to the surface. Repeat with another tone to produce a soft, brushy finish.

Getting started

*U*sing paint to create eye-catching designs need not be a complicated task that involves mastering new skills. All the different decorating ideas within this small child's room are easy to do.

Primary colours always look fresh and bright. Try printing with just your hand or finger for bold areas of colour, and use basic techniques such as spattering for more gentle, diffused effects. Notebooks, files, wastepaper bins or small boxes are excellent projects to begin with. You can paint the effects directly onto items such as storage boxes or apply them to paper and then use the paper as a decorative cover.

Simple friezes add interest to a child's room and are perfect for learning first colours. Here a frieze of houses drawn around building bricks makes a stimulating and attractive display.

Right *The frieze of houses is drawn around building blocks and brightly painted in primary colours. Photographs are displayed in mount board frames cut into house shapes.*

Below *Storage boxes decorated with lines painted into checks and spattering. Both these effects are easy to achieve.*

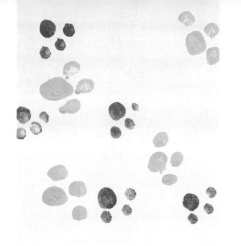

Far left Finger paint prints positioned as cat prints prowling across the toy box.

Left A toddler's hand print decorates another toy box.

FIRST STEPS

One of the advantages of these basic paint techniques is that there is no need to dash out and buy new equipment. Other than paint, all you need for many of the projects in this book arc art brushes, pencils and general decorating tools. The charming child's frieze featured here relies on toddlers' building blocks.

An endless variety of paint techniques is available to you and most of them are very easy to achieve with acrylic paint. The simplest techniques are often ignored in favour of more sophisticated-looking finishes, but with some thought basic paint ideas can look extremely effective.

PLANNING YOUR DECORATION

When you are unfamiliar with using paint and brushes even the easiest of techniques may seem rather daunting, especially when you have decided to decorate a whole room and are faced with large expanses of wall. It is a good idea, no matter how simple or complicated the project you wish to tackle, to test your ideas on white paper first; you can always use it up as wrapping paper.

Consider your wall and furniture areas carefully. Just a frieze or dado rail around a room can add impact and interest, or you may prefer to scatter an overall design on a piece of furniture or paint on a single motif. I always advise experimenting with small projects to begin with despite continually jumping in at the deep end myself.

BUILDING BLOCKS FRIEZE

This little room is divided with a low frieze suitable for the child's height, and to complement the child's bed. It consists of a long row of simple block houses, buildings and trees. I have used the same colours for balls painted in with the same primary colours and randomly placed underneath.

As an alternative to children's building blocks you could trace around paper cut-outs of items the child likes, such as sailing boats, dinosaurs or rabbits.

PHOTOGRAPH FRAMES

The wall decoration is completed by simple photograph frames cut out of card to reproduce the shapes of the buildings. They are painted with the same bright primary colours used for the frieze.

COORDINATING TOY BOXES

Basic hand and finger prints arc casy techniques to use for decorating plain items such as storage boxes. Simple finger prints can be placed to form animal paw prints and children especially enjoy the idea of using their hands as painting tools. I regret not having more nostalgic mementos of my children's toddler days, so a two-year-old friend and I had fun making hand prints. She found it amusing and now has a personalized toy box.

Other ideas include painting criss crossing lines into a bold check over a box or perhaps just across the corners as I have done. Spattering small dots of colour over the surface also looks effective.

I have painted all these boxes with these simple techniques, but the use of coordinated colours makes them look quite sophisticated. The colour circles beneath the frieze swirl in a random design and combine with the boxes to link the frieze to the play area.

STEP BY STEP
Building blocks frieze

This bright frieze is painted in acrylics and should be washable with a soft cloth, but as this is a child's room and walls are apt to need more attention, it is advisable to apply several coats of transparent varnish over the frieze to protect the surface.

MATERIALS

Acrylic paints (I used System 3) in
Ultramarine, Coeruleum, Lemon Yellow,
Cadmium Yellow, Cadmium Red, Crimson,
and a combination of Lemon Yellow
and Coeruleum to create green

•

Pencil

•

Spirit level

•

Children's building blocks

•

Art brush

•

Eraser

•

Acrylic varnish

1 Draw a horizontal line along the wall at the base height of the frieze (use a spirit level for this rather than measuring from the bottom of the wall, as floors are notoriously uneven). Using a pencil, lightly draw around a block for the base of the house, then use a triangular block for the roof. The trees are made from cylinders and the spires from elongated triangles.

2 Using acrylic straight from the tube, paint in evenly each colour block. Progress along the frieze painting all the shapes you wish to be in one colour, then rinse your brush and then paint in other blocks using another colour. Finish the frieze by combining a little Coeruleum with Lemon Yellow to create a fresh green and paint in the tree tops with a swirl of paint.

3 Draw around a cylinder beneath the frieze, clustering some circles together and leaving larger spaces between others. The swirls of colour will look as natural as bubbles blowing in the wind, or balls thrown into the air. Fill the brush with paint and squeeze it against the wall; then, following the circle line, swirl the colour around in a single movement.

4 For the finishing touch to the frieze add small strokes of paint for grass growing between the houses, linking the frieze along the wall. Wait until the wall is completely dry, and then rub out the pencil markings. Varnish to protect your handiwork. Truly transparent non-yellowing varnish can be difficult to obtain, so make a test on white paper first before applying an unknown varnish to a bright white wall.

19

Basic paint techniques

Simple decorations can be adapted to all sorts of surfaces and items. The primary colours I have used coordinate with the building blocks frieze, but these designs can be varied in numerous combinations of colours. Children of all ages will enjoy trying out these techniques.

MATERIALS

Acrylic paints (I used System 3) in Ultramarine, Cadmium Yellow and Crimson

•

Flat art brushes

•

Toothbrush

2 Wipe one colour off before you change to the next and repeat as much as you like. I can assure you that you will tire long before the two year old, so either have plenty of projects to cover or lots of spare paper to hand.

HAND PRINTS

1 Hand painting is much easier with a two-year-old child if you hold the paint for them. Paint their hand and let them plonk it onto the box. Then re-paint again for each print required.

FINGER PAINTING

Finger prints are fun to do and your imagination can turn them into the gentlest of pets or a fierce wild animal on the prowl. Just dip your finger into the paint and print. Individual prints look stunning over a large area and the effect can be surprisingly chic. Try them in vertical or horizontal rows. The amusing thing is that most people looking at the pattern do not realize the soft dots are finger prints.

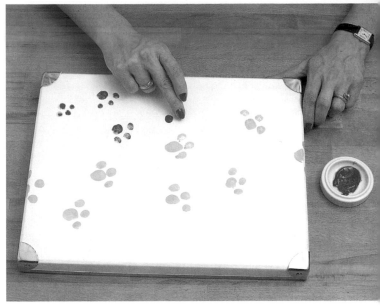

PAINTED STRIPES

Stripes and checks painted with a flat brush can be subtle or bold depending or how much colour you use on your brush and the width of the brush. Very watery acrylic stripes can traverse one another giving wonderful translucent effects. Slightly overlap arches of colour to form a rainbow, or use soft colours to design a smart checked pattern over a box as here.

SPATTERING

Spatter painting gives very varied effects. Here I have used a toothbrush over a shallow box. On a larger expanse of wall a stiff scrubbing brush and thick rubber gloves would be more appropriate. An apron is essential for this technique! First cover a wide area with newspaper, or work on a washable surface. Mask out any areas that you do not wish to decorate. Place the brush into a watery solution of paint and, with the bristles downwards, drag your finger over the bristles, releasing the paint in spatters over your work. Experiment with the height at which you hold your brush – the higher the brush, the more diffused the effect.

21

Colour and the palette

People are often confused about how to use colours and particularly nervous about mixing their own colours. I rely on a very simple colour palette of six acrylic paint colours, which are very easy to mix to produce further colours, plus black and white. My trick is, instead of choosing just three primary colours of red, blue and yellow, I take two of each primary hue, each with a slight bias towards another primary colour.

The two reds I use are Crimson, which has a hint of blue, and Cadmium Red, with a hint of yellow; the two yellows are Cadmium Yellow, with a red bias, and Lemon Yellow, which has a blue bias; the two blues are Coeruleum, with a touch of yellow in it and Ultramarine, which leans towards red.

MIXING COLOURS

To produce clear colours you need to mix hues that harmonize with each other. Mixing Cadmium Red, for instance, which has a hint of yellow, with Cadmium Yellow, which has a hint of red, gives a vibrant orange. However, if you were to use the wrong red, the Crimson, with the Cadmium Yellow, then the orange mixed would be darker and duller because of the hint of blue in the Crimson. I water down my acrylic paints as required to achieve either an intense or thinner colourwashed effect.

COLOUR CHART TABLE TOP

The table top is a small sample of thirteen bright colours mixed out of my six colours. The important lesson is to understand how to repeat a certain shade and with the simple method used here you will be able to mix your colours again and again.

All the furniture in my teenage daughter's room was very inexpensive and we assembled it ourselves at home. Before we could paint it the finish of the wood needed fine sandpapering and then a light coat of clear satin acrylic varnish to

Left *An inexpensive table top transformed into a dazzling colour chart from six primary colours.*

seal the surface. I always use this varnish as it is water soluble, odourless and colourless, so it does not affect the finished tone of the work.

With my six acrylic colours and several brushes I painted small squares of pure and mixed colour. The first square was Cadmium Yellow. Then I mixed some Cadmium Yellow with a little Cadmium Red to make a light orange and used this colour to paint one square above the yellow patch and one on each side of it, making a triangular shape. I positioned another Cadmium Yellow square at a diagonal to the first and continued

working in the same colours, traversing the table top until reaching the opposite side. I added further colours at the sides so that the whole of the table was eventually covered. I did not use masking tape to guide me and you will find that it is fairly easy to work by eye. You may make a mistake here or there – I produced the odd wiggle towards the far corner of the table – but this does not spoil the effect. When the table was thoroughly dry I coated it with several light layers of varnish for protection.

25

Left *Swirls of tones decorate the stool, visually linking it to the table.*

Right *Small chests of drawers tuck practically below the table. This one is decorated in cool tones of green, into yellow, through to blue.*

Below *A progression of tones ranging from yellows and oranges through to reds.*

ARTIST'S STOOL

The artist's stool is painted in warm rings of Cadmium Yellow through to Crimson, then coated with varnish. It is easy to tackle by first lightly marking the outlines of the circles in pencil, measuring from the centre with different lengths of string.

MULTI-COLOURED CHESTS OF DRAWERS

The chests of drawers also needed to be sanded down before being painted. They are decorated in cool greens to blue and hot yellow through to red, always naturally blending and relating one colour to another. The simple geometric motifs are then stencilled on. You will find it easier to remove the knobs before painting the drawers.

Stencilling geometric shapes

Stencilling is quick, easy and fun to do and simple geometric
designs cut out of paper can transform even the smallest drawers.
For an interesting and less predictable effect, vary the positions
of the shapes as well as the colour combinations.

MATERIALS

Cartridge paper

•

Scissors

•

Acrylic paints

•

Stencil brush

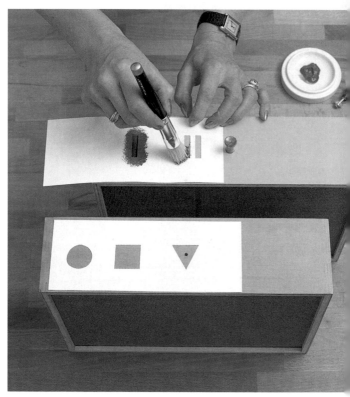

1 The simplest form of stencil can be cut from
white cartridge paper. Fold the paper in half and
cut the forms that you like, then open out the
paper to give the full shape. Any shapes that are
not symmetrical, such as the triangle, can be cut
out directly with a pair of scissors.

2 Hold your stencil in position on the drawer.
Use a very small amount of paint on the brush and
work it well into the bristles. Stencil gently with a
light tapping motion to release the paint from the
brush. Here Coeruleum blue is stencilled onto the
Lemon Yellow drawer.

3 Stencil each drawer with a different combination of colours; for instance, paint Cadmium Yellow over the Ultramarine drawer. Place the shapes in different positions on each drawer. I painted a circle over the hole drilled for one of the knobs.

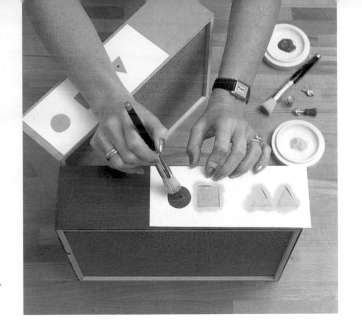

4 Remove the stencil carefully, by lifting it up from one corner and peeling it away, making sure that you do not smudge the paint. Paint the drawer knobs in contrasting colours.

5 When the paint is dry apply a coat of varnish to the drawers for additional protection. Allow this to dry before replacing the drawer knobs, screwing them firmly into position.

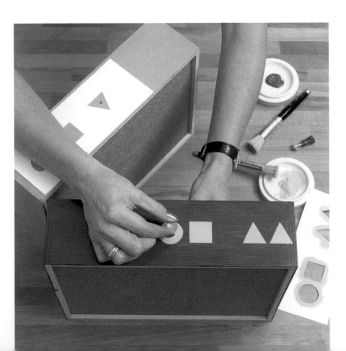

29

Painting checks onto the walls

Painting directly onto the walls is a dramatic and easy way to create a pattern. Just paint over your guidelines and any wall space will take on a new look. Plan your design on a small scale on paper if you are uncertain.

MATERIALS

Plumb line

•

Wide paintbrush

•

Medium paintbrush

•

Narrow paintbrush

•

Tape measure or ruler

•

Low-tack masking tape

•

Set square or protractor

•

Diluted acrylic paints in
Cadmium Red and Coeruleum

1 Suspend a plumb line down the wall so that you have a straight line to follow from the ceiling. If you do not have one you can improvise by hanging anything weighty from a piece of string. Using a fairly wide brush paint a stripe down the wall in a firm stroke; paint directly over the string and repeat the line if the paint is not strong enough. My stripe is in Cadmium Red.

2 Measure up from the skirting board, and place low-tack masking tape along the desired horizontal line. Check your measurements carefully and make sure that the plumb line falls at a 90 degree angle to the masking tape. In older houses the floor can curve, so step well back to check that the masking tape looks straight to the eye.

3 With a medium size brush and contrasting paint (I used Coeruleum), paint along the masking tape. Be sure to remove the tape before the paint is dry as you do not want the paint to seal the masking tape to the wall.

4 My brush became a little wispy and left stray marks. If this happens simply go over any unwanted marks with your original wall colour to hide them. Use a narrow brush for this as it will give you more control.

CONFIDENT COLOUR ON WALLS

My daughter is now attending art school and instead of pretty pastels and delicate floral patterns, strong bold lines, colours and effects are required. So, under her direction, we painted the walls of her room a powerful warm yellow with contrasting cool blue woodwork. Confident Cadmium Red stripes were painted down the wall with Coeruleum blue lines crossing them to make a checked pattern.

Abigail's own illustration of colour relationships using complementary colours is framed in red and her artwork of colour harmonies framed in blue. Her lessons intrigue me and without her encouragement I would not have had the confidence to use such intense colours. So do have a go! The decoration of her study bedroom really works. The room is interesting to look at and supports her energy, music, clothes and clutter very well. I hasten to add that the other walls are a lighter tone of yellow, rather less over-powering to wake up to in the morning.

Dots and sprigs

Smaller projects are most rewarding, but do not necessarily mean less work. Often painting interesting shapes such as an oval tray or clock face involves adapting design templates, and even a rectangular tray has to be carefully measured. The more familiar you become with a template the more variation you will be able to plan, perhaps painting just one ivy leaf as if it has fallen onto a shelf, for instance, or a long ivy trail around a clock.

Simple dots painted as a linear pattern or as a scatter motif design over furniture or walls can produce some stunning effects. They can be used individually or contained in clusters within a specified area. Equally, basic sponging in a combination of colours can provide an effective backdrop to your painted furniture.

Sponging

Use a sea sponge for this paint effect as it gives a soft, natural look.
Dampen it so that it assumes its full size before dipping it in the
paint. I mixed Coeruleum with Lemon Yellow to produce a leaf
green colour, then oversponged with Coeruleum.

MATERIALS

Acrylic paints in Coeruleum and
Lemon Yellow

•

A natural sea sponge

•

Paintbrush for mixing

•

Kitchen paper

1 Sponging is one of the easiest paint techniques,
providing you test the sponge each time that you
have reloaded it with paint. If the sponge is
overloaded you will leave a large splodge on the
wall. So test beforehand and dab the sponge lightly.

2 Continue lightly tapping the sponge against the wall, building up the sponge effect as you proceed.

3 Sponge over areas that look a little bare. Stand well back from the wall to judge the overall effect.

4 Adding a touch of contrasting blue, the sponging was given more tone. With sponging you can decide the effect as you go along, or return to build it up another day.

35

RECTANGULAR TRAY

Interweaving sprigs and dots can be used in many ways. I originally saw this design in blue on a white cup, and adapted it for a rectangular tray, extending the sprigs' stalks to add interest and movement to the corners. There is a template of this design for you to follow at the back of the book. Transfer the design onto the tray with a pencil using tracing paper or use tracing paper with a layer of carbon paper underneath. Then

paint in the design following the pencil outlines. This is a very easy method.

I also painted one or two napkin rings in coordinating Ultramarine dots.

OVAL TRAYS

Measuring and calculating to accurately place designs that link into corners or continue the design flow, as in the oval trays, can become a nightmare. So I usually cheat and cut a piece of

Opposite *Fresh blue and white breakfast tray decorated with intertwining sprigs and dots.*

Above *This smart red and black tray shows another variation for the placement of the dot and sprig design.*

Left *Just simple dots in a carefully planned design can create an elegant tray for serving evening drinks.*

tracing paper to fit inside the tray. Removing it from the tray, I then fold the tracing paper into quarters and work out the pattern for one quarter by sliding the template underneath to see how it works. By pushing the template up and down under the quarter shape you will find where it fits naturally without leaving gaps or have your design doubling up. This method is easier than it sounds and will ensure the successful continuation of your design around the tray.

With the red tray I marked out the arches and decided to fill them in. I mirror-imaged the sprig design onto the red base and just painted in an oval of dots as a central design.

I altered the design slightly for the white tray, filling in the same traced oval in the centre with dots and using dots again for the same arch markings that curve delicately around the edge. As a result the white tray looks completely different from the red one.

FREEHAND SPRIG CLOCK

A variety of clock faces are available in kit form
and give endless possibilities for decoration.

Apply several coats of white paint. Place a small
piece of masking tape over the central hole where
the movement will be connected. With a compass,
draw two circles for the clock face where you will
place the numerals. Trace out the numerals onto
the clock using a protractor to accurately place
them – at 30 degrees if you want to put in all
twelve numbers or at 90 degrees for just the four
quarter ones. Some more cheating – you have to be
very accurate with a brush to achieve beautiful
numbers, so I colour mine in with felt tips. I have
bought an adapter for my compass to hold a felt-tip
pen and that has enabled me to obtain accurate
lines to delineate my clock face.

For the blue clock I drew some freehand sprig
lines that are easy for you to copy and added some
yellow dots as stylized berries. When, however, I
tried to varnish the clock face using thin acrylic
varnish, I smudged the felt-tip pen lines, as you can
see around the numeral three. So, for the rest of
the clock I used a spray can varnish and you may
find this method more successful.

Connect the movement to your clock following
the instructions that come with the kit.

IVY DESIGNS

The ivy clock on page 32 was quite time
consuming to paint, with all twelve numbers and
the intricate ivy design. I mirror-imaged the design
around the square supporting the clock face, while
an ivy sprig nestles in the arch. There is a template
for you to follow at the back of the book.

The two photograph frames on page 39 are
lightly colourwashed with green, with ivy forming
an arch over one frame and placed in opposite
corners on the other.

Above *Trailing ivy adds interest to these green colourwashed photograph frames.*

Left above *Quickly applied freehand blue brush strokes decorate this white clock, with yellow dots added for fun.*

Left *A detailed shot of the blue and white clock shows just how easily these strokes of paint are placed.*

Painted rocking horse

Twelve years ago I found this wonderful 1860s wooden rocking horse mounted on a traditional bow and bought it for my young daughter. Since then hc has been greatly loved, ridden and abused and eventually stood looking rather lame and the worse for wear in a corner.

We took him to be restored, had every joint repaired and new ears carved. But we wanted to paint him ourselves, so the restorers told us the secrets of painting old wood like this to give a traditional look. While my daughter consulted a book to choose the horse's markings, I set to work on preparing the surface of the wood.

You can use the method I describe here, of filling in irregularities with gesso and plaster of Paris, for preparing similar old toys and pieces of furniture for repainting.

Restoring the rocking horse

Before we could start decorating the horse I had to make sure that
the surface was sound and smooth for repainting. Gesso and plaster
of Paris were used widely by artists in the Middle Ages and
Renaissance for preparing wooden surfaces.

MATERIALS

Gesso

•

Plaster of Paris

•

Wide paintbrush

•

Sandpaper (medium and fine grades)

•

Acrylic paints in Crimson,
Cadmium Yellow and Coeruleum mixed
to make a warm brown, and Black

•

Art brush

•

Stencil brush

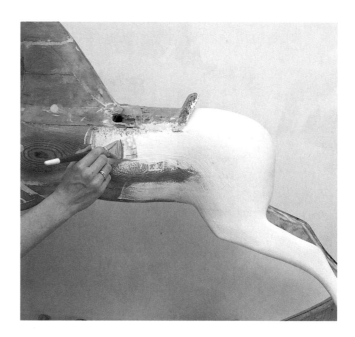

1 Paint the raw wood with a thick layer of gesso
mixed with sifted plaster of Paris in the ratio
of about 1 tablespoon of gesso to 1 teaspoon of
plaster of Paris. Cover all unwanted irregularities
with the mixture and keep it airtight.

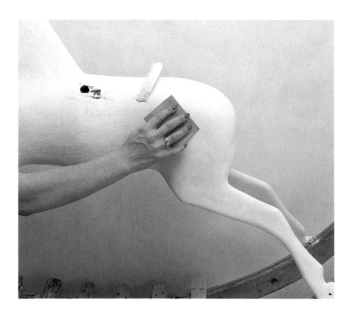

2 Be very patient and sand down the dried
surface with small pieces of sandpaper, curving
them within your fingers to take account of the
horse's curves.

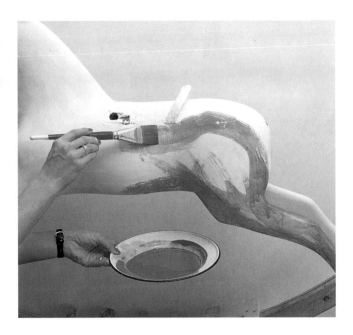

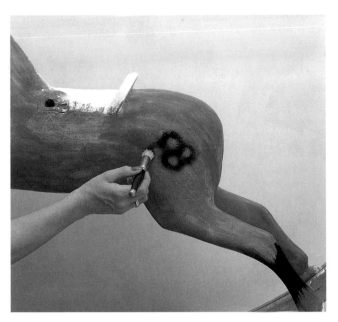

3 Make up a wash of colour and cover the horse completely with the paint.

5 Using a stencil brush, create dapples. Stencil over them more densely in the middle and diffuse the dapples out over the horse's hindquarters.

4 The details give character to the horse. I wanted natural and diffused markings although we took artistic licence with his 'breed'. Paint in the hooves and leg markings in black.

6 Gently shade in the lower tummy. Paint the ears and nostril, and shade in the facial muscle. Some traditional rocking horses also have red inside the mouth, inner nostril and ears, but we settled for brown. As a finishing touch we painted his saddle bright red. Finally, varnish well and be prepared to repaint again once children begin riding him!

Summer flowers

*I*t is easy to create a harmonious room by repeating a simple theme using delicate applications of paint. The gentle roses and ribbons effects shown here are achieved with diluted acrylic paints used like watercolours.

This small bedroom feels calm and relaxing – just the place to snuggle into bed with a good book. Light sprays of roses decorate the drawers of the bedside chest, while a stem tied with a ribbon is painted as if left on the surface. There are translucent roses on the paper lampshade and bunches of roses, buds and hips seem to be hung to dry on the screen. Tight ribbon bows are tucked into the corners of the headboard. There are so many ways to use these charming designs to enhance your furniture.

Using acrylics for 'watercolour' ribbons

This 'watercolour' technique of painting can only be achieved when
the furniture is placed laying down flat. Most furniture can be
placed on its side so this presents no problem; for instance, take out
the drawers from a chest to have a flat work surface.

MATERIALS

Template at back of book
•
Acrylic paints in Coeruleum,
Cadmium Yellow and Crimson
•
Art brushes (I used Dalon D77,
sizes 5 and 8)
•
Water
•
Tracing paper
•
Pencil
•
Yellow or white crayon
(for dark furniture)

1 Using the templates at the back of the book,
trace out in pencil the part of the design that suits
the furniture you are decorating. The blue bow looked
charming tucked into the corner of the headboard,
but I decided to extend the ribbon design to make
the bedhead look softer in appearance. You will need
to trace the design on the wrong side of the tracing
paper first so that your pencil lines are transferred.

2 Peel back your tracing pattern to reveal the pencil outlines beneath. If your furniture is dark use a yellow or white crayon on the reverse of the tracing for a clearer image.

3 The 'watercolour' technique is achieved by creating a pool of water in each outlined area, into which the paint is then dropped. The shaded areas of the templates show areas where the paint colours will be more intense. Fill each ribbon section individually with a water-laden brush.

4 For the ribbons dip the brush into the acrylic Coeruleum straight from the tube, and place the loaded brush gently along the side of the water pool. Paint will immediately diffuse out into the pool, creating a wonderful gradation of colour.

BEDSIDE CHEST OF DRAWERS

Both the chest of drawers and bed were bought inexpensively. They had a high yellow pine finish, but a softer, slightly more natural effect was quickly accomplished by sanding the furniture down and applying an undercoat of deep pink followed by several watered-down layers of white emulsion paint.

The rose template at the back of the book is designed to be used as you like, pruning away parts of it or using it as a repeat pattern; you could paint a complete bouquet of flowers by repeating the spray of rose hips, buds and flowers.

I placed just the spray of roses on the front of the drawers, with the stem curve nestling under the knob. By flipping over the tracing template a mirror image gives a symmetrical design. On the top surface I painted a sprig of roses tied with a trailing ribbon. The tracing paper templates at the back of the book have been designed so that the bow and ribbon design interlinks with the roses,

buds and hips pattern. By placing one tracing template over the other you will see the variations possible for your own pieces of furniture. Trace through your composition omitting the part of the stem that will be tied by the bow, as I have done for the decoration on the top of the chest of drawers.

When you are painting the rose design keep each petal pool separate; this will give a fine, transfused quality to the flower. Complete each petal in the same way as described for the ribbons on page 46, using Crimson paint. To give a centre to the open rose, place into it a brush of Cadmium Yellow; this will also diffuse out into the base of the petals, giving a natural effect.

You can make a muted rose leaf green by mixing Cadmium Yellow and Coeruleum; the more yellow you add the lighter your green and the more blue you add the darker your green will be. Experiment with different tones.

Opposite *Delicately applied, the roses add subtle charm to any setting. An uncluttered, simple look works well in coordinating the pieces in this bedroom.*

Left *Combining the ribbon template with the rose design allows further decorative possibilities.*

FOLDING SCREEN

My daughter loves to change the position of her furniture and, sharing a room with her younger sister, a folding screen acts as a useful divider for clothes strewn on the floor and can shield light for anyone who wishes to read late into the night. It is also perfect to divide the two varying styles within the same room.

The screen on page 44 is constructed of basic thin hardboard on a wooden frame and to prepare the surface I covered it with watered-down white emulsion paint applied quickly with bold brush strokes.

As the screen is a large area, I enlarged the rose design onto A3 paper. If you have a friendly photocopying shop take your own A3 tracing paper in and ask the shop to place it in the photocopier paper tray and you can immediately have your image ready for use on tracing paper; if not you will have to trace it out.

I dry a lot of flowers and so I decided to reverse the design on the screen so that it looked like bunches hanging upside down, painting them with the same method used for the other pieces in the room. I might just add a real nail to make them look more real.

BED HEADBOARD

Small ribbons tucked into the corners of the headboard make a restful composition and complement the soft linen of the pillows. My original idea was to have lots of trailing ribbons with scattered roses, but in the end I decided that a more restrained design looked more effective. If you want to add more flowers later, there is no problem; acrylic paint allows you to paint over a final coat of varnish to expand the design.

Opposite *A twisted repeat of the ribbon design decorates the headboard.*

Left *The painted paper lampshade coordinates with the furniture, adding warmth as the light transfuses through the paper petals.*

PAPER LAMPSHADE

Creating a coordinated look to a room need not be expensive. Bedside lampshades are always getting bumped, whether last thing at night as a sleepy hand turns off the light or first thing in the morning when switching it on, so they seem to need replacing frequently. To lower my costs, I took an old lampshade off the metal support frame and used it as a pattern to cut out a new one.

For the new shade in my daughter's bedroom I chose 200 gsm watercolour paper as I like the texture. You can find a selection of suitable papers with a wide variety of colours and textures in good art suppliers.

Using the template, plan a design that suits your lamp; I chose the roses with buds, tracing out the flowers. I painted the lampshade using the same 'watercolour' method as for the drawer front.

When the paint is thoroughly dry, gently rub out any pencil marks, and protect the shade with a spray fixative available from art suppliers. Bend the shade around the metal support and glue down the overlapping edge; paperclips will help temporarily to hold it in the curved position. Lightly apply glue to the top of the metal support and place the shade over the top.

VARNISHING YOUR FURNITURE

Protect all your painted furniture with several layers of varnish; the top of the chest of drawers or surface of any similar piece will require more coats than the screen or headboard. As the roses and ribbons decoration produced a subtle effect I used a dead flat varnish, so that the paint finish would not alter. Many varnishes are readily available, so take care in selecting the finish you want.

Above *These pretty hexagonal boxes are all decorated with different elements taken from the templates at the back of the book. They are ideal for hiding oddments in.*

Right *The design on the small shelf is linked by crossing the two stems.*

Opposite *Pink-stippled clock, decorated with small elements from the rose template.*

52

HEXAGONAL BOXES

Small boxes are useful for oddments that you want to keep to hand in the bedroom but prefer to be out of sight.

Each box is coated in base white and then stippled in two tones of colour. The tissue box decorated with a yellow bow is stippled in blue, then restippled in green. The delicate blue box with trailing rose and leaves is restippled with a touch of grey, and the smallest box with sprigs of rose hips is stippled in yellow with a further coat of palest grey stippling.

ROSES CLOCK AND SMALL SHELF

Just the use of small elements of the whole rose design can look charming. Reversing the rose hips and crossing the stems beneath the clock or using the rose with reversed rosebuds each side accentuates the 'crown' of the clock. For how to paint in the clock face and numerals see the instructions for the freehand sprig clock on page 38.

The design on the small shelf, which is decorated on two dimensions, is linked by the flower stems crossing. For pieces like this make

sure that you arrange the design so that the main flower is not folded. I have used just the roses for the back of the shelf and the ribbon and rose hip design for the shelf itself so that the eye moves around the curved shape of the shelf.

DAISY CHAINS

Used as individual flower heads or threaded into a chain, daisies are always a delight. The daisy chain template at the back of the book can be repeated or reversed to make any number of patterns. Just as it is easy to make a slit in the last real daisy to continue the chain as long as you require, so you can paint a slitted effect in long strings of flowers to suit your furniture or walls.

DAISY DESIGNS

On the green dragged tray I have used the daisies in a continuous pattern, overlapping the stalks. You will see that I have also painted slits in the stalks so that the daisies swirl in a natural-looking chain, taking the eye around the tray.

The lightly brushed yellow pen tidy and stationery holder are also adorned with daisies. Reversing the daisies back and forth gives the flowers additional movement.

Sometimes keeping the design as simple as possible can have more effect when painting these familiar meadow flowers. When decorating the rush chair I deliberately painted in only a few single daisies.

Opposite *An intertwined daisy chain twirls around the tray in a fairly haphazard design.*

Left *Daisy heads complement the country style of this rush-seated chair. You could also adapt the design to paint blue cornflowers.*

Below *Here the daisy motif has been adapted to decorate a stationery holder and pen tidy to make the task of letter writing a delight.*

Painting a daisy chair

Wild flowers give a fresh, country look to plain rush-seated chairs.
I have used just three daisies at the top of the chair and one along
the middle slat that looks as if it is about to be joined into a chain.

MATERIALS

Template at back of book

•

Acrylic paints in Lemon Yellow,
Cadmium Yellow, Coeruleum,
Crimson and White

•

Art brushes (sizes 6 and 00)

•

Tracing paper

•

2B pencil

1 Using the template at the back of the book,
trace out the daisy design onto tracing paper with
a soft 2B pencil. Reverse the tracing so that the
pencil side touches the wooden slats of the chair.
Then press through, going over the template daisy
outlines to leave a pencil image on top of the chair.

2 Go over any pencil lines that seem faint, then
reposition the template to trace out a daisy along
the middle slat.

3 Paint in the white petals from tip to centre. Not only do I steady the chair with one hand, but my wrist rests on the chair. Resting on my little finger also helps to support my painting hand.

5 Combine a touch of Coeruleum with Lemon Yellow to make a leaf green and paint in the stems.

4 Dot in the centre of the daisies, first with Lemon Yellow, then add a few dots of Cadmium Yellow to add depth.

6 For the finishing detail combine white with Crimson to make pink and with a tiny brush paint in the tips of each petal. By keeping your brush very dry you can produce a dragged effect that will resemble the natural-looking marks seen on real daisies.

3 Mask out the pencilled-line panel frame, curving the tape accurately to the corners. Paint the wall with either a prepared paint glaze or acrylic paint mixed with acrylic gel retarder (this stops the acrylic paint drying quickly and gives you more time to work).

4 With a gentle rocking, dragging motion, pull the plastic wood-grainer down the wall through the paint. The more pressure you apply the greater definition you will achieve. If you do not like a particular drag, just redrag over the false mark and have another go. Wood is not uniform in grain, so the greater the variance, the better the effect. It is probably better to complete the whole piece first. Do not analyze it too much and you will be surprised how successful a larger expanse of wood graining looks.

5 Paint in the panel frame with an art brush. Add a further depth of tone to the side of the panel frame that touches the wood graining; this will give the illusion of the panelling being slightly raised rather than dead flat.

Lemons and leaves

Fresh bright lemons evoke a summer's day, their brilliance seeming to capture every moment snatched in the sun. I picked my first lemon last year and I have transferred the wonderful vibrant colour and profusion of fruit as I reached into the deep green twisting leaves onto the decoration of this simple metal café table and chairs.

The delight of lemon trees is that both the fruit and the delicate flowers that smell so exquisite are out at the same time, so my design has reflected this, with intertwining leaves, flowers and lemons encircling the table top. Slatted wooden chairs complete the set of outdoor furniture. A small tray complements the table and chairs with simple sprigs of lemons tucked into the corners.

METAL CAFÉ TABLE

This table is quite old and used continually throughout the summer by all the family. As it is our only outdoor table some of the uses to which it is put are quite unconventional and as a result the previous decoration of découpage began to be the worse for wear. After peeling the paint, stripping and finally sandpapering the metal surface back to the smoothest I could, I repainted the table top twice in a white base coat. I applied a light colourwash of Coeruleum over the white in random strokes, criss-crossing the surface. This left the white base coat showing through and gave a good surface on which to paint the lemon motifs.

60

Opposite *I have reversed the single lemon template to create a symmetrical design around the edge of the table.*

Left *Lemons painted in the corners of the tray coordinate it with its setting.*

Below *Again I have reversed the lemon templates at the back of the book, creating a colourful wall frieze with light applications of paint.*

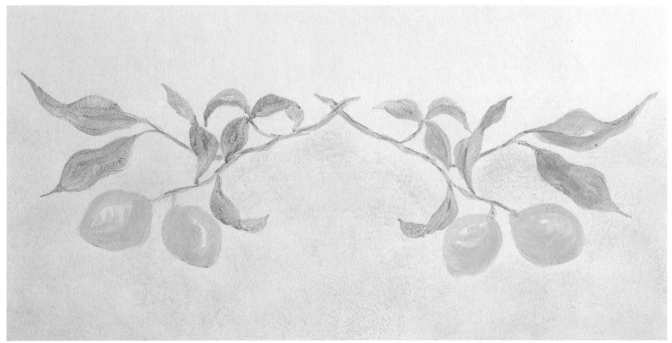

61

Right *Folding chairs are easy to stack and store and give endless possibilities for painted decoration.*

Opposite *A tray decorated with cool lemons is perfect for carrying drinks to quench summer thirst.*

APPLYING THE DESIGN

Transfer the template image of the lemons from the back of the book. Either trace it with pencil using tracing paper or use carbon paper underneath the tracing paper for a firmer outline. Place the lemon design in position and press firmly through the two layers.

The lemons can be placed all around the table top or in a heap by overlapping them, or put in ones or twos as 'place mats' where people sit. I have used them in full force bordering the table's edge. Vary the use of the templates; they can be repeated as a continuous motif, cutting leaves off a branch or joining more on. By sliding the two lemon templates over one another you will be able to create your own arrangements; it is easy to extend the stem by drawing a little beyond the design. Also use the mirror image of the designs; the single lemon template reversed with both stems crossing is perfect for a place setting.

When painting the design have a damp cloth to hand, so that if you apply too much paint you can gently dab a little off for a lighter feel without having to begin again.

WOODEN CHAIRS

I applied the same base coat of white to the wooden chair slats, then dragged Coeruleum smoothly and evenly across each slat.

You can use the lemons individually on the chair backs or as a whole lemon branch spanned over the chair seats, breaking the design but adding charm and individuality to each chair. The small flowers could also be used as an overall scatter design.

LEMONS TRAY

The plain wooden tray has also been given a base coat of white, then dragged with Lemon Yellow paint before applying the design. I chose to place a pair of lemons in two corners.

Painting the lemons and leaves

The clear yellows and greens of the lemons and their leaves
are enhanced by painting the decoration onto a Coeruleum
blue background that has been dragged or colourwashed onto
the furniture. The method for decorating the table is as
described here for the chairs.

MATERIALS

Templates at back of book

•

Acrylic paints in Coeruleum, Lemon Yellow,
Cadmium Yellow and White (also Cadmium Red
if you wish the branches to be brown)

•

Art brushes (sizes 4 and 6)

•

Varnish

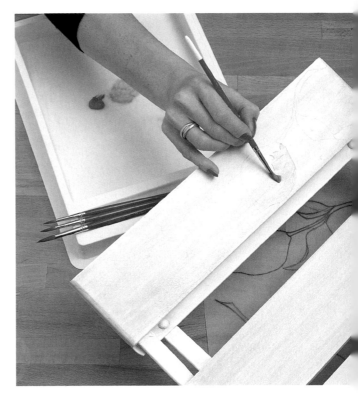

1 Apply the lemon's shading by mixing a little
Lemon Yellow and Coeruleum together, then
water it down to a lighter tone and test your
colour on kitchen paper. Lightly apply the paint
to the outside edge of the lemon, gently dragging
the green shading slightly into the lemon from
the reserve of paint in the initial brush stroke.
Start with a very small amount of paint, as you
can always add an additional layer. If you apply
too much at first you will have to wipe all the
paint away with a damp cloth and start again.

2 Using a slightly thicker application of Lemon Yellow, paint in the whole lemon. Let your brush strokes flow around the natural curves of the rounded lemon, as these brush marks will enhance the roundness of the fruit.

3 Mix a combination of Lemon Yellow with Coeruleum for varying tones of green for the leaves; the more yellow the lighter the green, the more blue the darker the green. Stroke on the paint in the same direction of the veins on the marked template; this will give your leaves natural movement.

4 Paint in the twig in green. Then mix a little Cadmium Red into the green to form a brown and gently introduce the brown over the green twig, reflecting the natural changing tones within a twig. Protect both the table top, legs, chairs and tray with several layers of varnish.

STEP BY STEP

Painted lemon frieze

Painting lemons into a frieze makes an ideal decoration for a conservatory or garden room used for summer eating and entertainment. The design coordinates with the metal café table, chairs and tray, and could be adapted to larger pieces of furniture.

MATERIALS

Templates at back of book

•

Acrylic paints in Coeruleum, Lemon Yellow, Cadmium Yellow and White (also Cadmium Red if you wish the branches to be brown)

•

Art brushes (sizes 10 and 12)

•

Tracing paper or carbon paper

•

Pencil

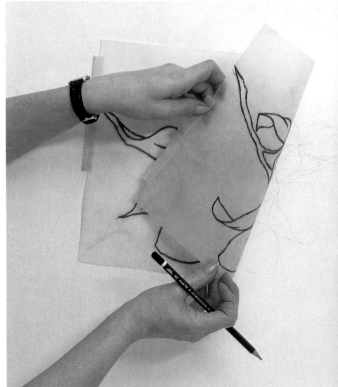

1 Enlarge the image on a photocopier and trace it out onto tracing paper. Using the tracing paper template, transfer your design along a measured horizontal line across the wall. To facilitate positioning the design draw a soft central line onto the lemon tracing, then simply place the line on the tracing over the lightly marked line on the wall. This will avoid the necessity for further measuring.

2 To achieve a watery, mellow look for the wall frieze in contrast to the neater painting on the metal café table, I used a larger brush and watered down the paint for softer hues of the same colours.

4 Mixing a little Coeruleum with Lemon Yellow achieves a subtle green that can be painted over the areas of shading to bring life to the flat yellow. Paint in the green leaves.

3 Paint in all the lighter areas in yellow, remembering to leave the odd dash white as a highlight. I find very free painting quite difficult, so I just keep painting and only after I have completely finished a branch do I look at my work with a critical eye. I can then add more paint or dab some off with a damp cloth if I wish.

5 Adding more blue to form a darker green paint mix, paint in veins to the leaves and texture to the stalk. Rub out all pencil lines left uncovered.

Designs
with lines

*O*ne of the most effective ways of decorating walls or furniture is to accentuate outlines or to place lines so that they divide up a large surface. I needed a piece of furniture in which to store all my artwork and papers and as my workroom is shared with my son when he is home from college, furniture must be adaptable and not look too designed for office or art use. On finding a dilapidated piece dating from around 1900 painted in battleship grey, the remains of a pot used on the many pleasure and fishing boats requisitioned for use in World War II, I imagined a bright, well-restored and versatile piece of furniture for my daily work use. But this piece of furniture had other surprises in store for me.

WORK CHEST

Never restore an old piece of furniture if you are feeling faint-hearted. I was in excellent spirits when I started this project, but when the three days I had put aside for it turned into two weeks certain compromises with the piece were made. The smart chic look that I had envisaged became more of a rustic, bohemian effect.

There were many problems. Each job I set myself took double the time I had planned, and several other jobs that I had not even anticipated surfaced. First I found that I could not remove the handles. Then I found that stripping paint from a piece with fifteen drawers was extremely time consuming, though it was an interesting surprise as the old paint slid away under the palette knife to note the classic Arts and Crafts movement stencil *c.*1890–1900 swirling up the sides.

The wooden sides were badly damaged, however, and needed a great deal of sanding with an electric sander. The vibrations of the sander shook most of the interior shelf supports loose, which was when I discovered that woodworm had had a field day. I applied liberal coats of woodworm fluid over and into the holes and then found that the paint would not adhere to the oils in the previously applied woodworm treatment, so I was back to sanding each and every surface again. Have I put you off restoring old pieces of furniture yet? I shall re-read this passage if I am tempted by another piece – and I know I will be, I always am!

USING MASKING TAPE

The technique for using masking tape is very simple. The base coat of paint will be the colour of the line, the top coat of paint will be the main covering colour of the furniture or wall. Thus you can build up patterns with gradated tones.

Conventional masking tape can sometimes cause seepage or damage to the paintwork on the furniture, depending on the technique and type of paint you use. On expressing exasperation at this problem at my local art shop, a customer suggested I use Micropore, a tape used for medical dressings, and although it is expensive I now use this on all my projects. Another expensive alternative is photographic film tape. If you use ordinary masking tape you will probably have more success with the low-tack type.

PICTURE FRAMES

The frames were masked with tape to enhance the stripy theme in the room and painted in bright oranges, reds and contrasting blue.

Left *Experiment with different masking tapes. I had the most success with Micropore, which I used on the lower drawers of this chest.*

Opposite *Brightly painted clean lines are easily achieved on frames by using masking tape.*

Making designs on the workchest

You will achieve the best and most accurate result with Micropore, which is used to keep medical dressings in place. It is much more expensive than conventional masking tape, but well worth the cost and I have used it on the lower drawers of the workchest.

MATERIALS

Cutting mat
•
Craft knife or scalpel
•
Pencil
•
Straightedge
•
Masking tape or Micropore
•
Paintbrush
•
Acrylic paint in your
chosen colour
•
Varnish

1 Small masking lines are easy to achieve by sticking the tape down onto a cutting mat. Then mark your design in pencil and cut accurately against a straightedge with a cutting knife. I had reasonable success with low-tack masking tape, but normal masking tape removed some of the paint when it was peeled off, so I had to begin again.

2 Stick the small cube detail into the corner and smooth the Micropore running border gently into place around the drawer. Repositioning is easy as the tape can be used several times, so I was able to re-use it on drawers of the same depth.

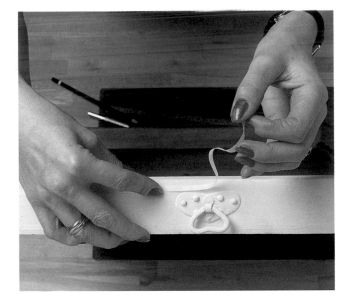

3 Paint over the top of the tape in your chosen contrasting colour. If you wish to build up several tones of colours use the lightest first and then paint over a mid tone; then position additional tape and paint the darker tone. When you lift the tapes you will have two differing tones showing. This alternative design was used for a diagonal pattern with differing widths of tape (I have shown an example on page 75.).

4 Peel away the tape to reveal the design beneath. Varnish all the surfaces of the furniture for additional protection.

WALL DESIGN

Having chosen a bright yellow colour for the workchest, I decided to paint the walls of the room in a complementary light Ultramarine and to try an effect that would seem to enlarge the room.

With masking tape you can create the illusion of panelling or painted lines and totally transform a room space into different proportions. Simply measure out the lines and place the tape on in the positions you require to break up a surface with diagonals and checks or to outline areas.

When you have decided on the pattern for your wall you may find it helpful to plan it on paper before putting the tape in position.

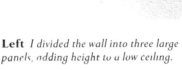

Left *I divided the wall into three large panels, adding height to a low ceiling.*

Top *Single thin tape applied in diagonals, then painted.*

Above *Ultramarine wash over a wall panel.*

Top *Preparation for a corner detail of a wall panel.*

Above *Thin masking tape is applied in diagonals, then painted. Thicker masking tape is applied over the thin, and the area painted in a darker tone.*

Masking the wall

The wall design is marked out in wide tape first, providing a
guide for the thinner tape line. I enlisted the help of my daughter
in marking out the walls; it is easier to work on large areas
with two people, but not essential.

MATERIALS

Tape measure or long metal rule

•

Spirit level

•

Pencil

•

Masking tape in wide and
narrow widths

•

Acrylic paint in your chosen
colour (I used Ultramarine)

•

Shallow paint container

•

Rubber gloves

•

Soft cloth

1 I divided this long, but not high-ceilinged, wall
into three large panels to enhance the height of the
room. Measuring the total wall area I divided it
into three, deciding on the area between the
panels – one at the end of the wall, the next two
between the panels and one at the far end of the
wall, so four spaces to deduct from my overall
measurement. Measure out soft, long pencil lines
using a long ruler and a spirit level so that you
achieve accurate vertical lines and then horizontal
lines for the top and bottom of the panel.

2 Mask to the edge of your line over the total
panel lines. There are different masking tapes
on the market; I used low-tack tape as my walls
are in poor condition and paint has been known
to fall off without much provocation. Ordinary
masking tape is preferable as it is cheaper and
allows for less seepage of paint underneath.

3 Choosing a thinner tape, use the previous measurements and the ruler to mark out the positioning for an interior panel or edging.

4 With both masking-tape panels in position and any small details you require for your decoration scheme, make a watery solution of acrylic paint in your chosen colour. Then apply the paint in a swirling movement all over the wall using a soft cloth. The high water content may encourage seepage under the tape. However, if you want crisp lines, use normal wall paint undiluted and apply it with stippling, rag rolling, or overall techniques that do not push the paint underneath the masking tape. Dragged paint would not seep on the verticals, but might seep under the horizontals; do a test run for paint consistency if you wish to avoid seepage.

5 This is the easy bit – just carefully peel off the masking tape. Gently does it if your walls are in bad shape.

Panelling and 3-D effects

Dividing up a wall area into different segments to form panels gives additional possibilities for interior decoration. The simplest white wall can be transformed into a panelled effect to give extra interest. The proportions of a room can be subtly changed; vertical lines always extend the height, while a strong dado line will reduce the height of a lofty room, the effect further emphasized if it is combined with a picture rail. Panels can be adapted to any size or shape; though usually rectangular they can look stunning in large diamond shapes, or as a semi-circle over the top of a door.

Similarly, 3-D details can be painted onto furniture and walls to give added impact. Small motifs can sometimes be worked up to create an almost *trompe l'œil* effect.

Opposite *The look of the room is totally changed by transforming a plain wall into a panelled one. The top panel is painted with defused dragging, while the lower one has wood graining applied to it.*

Left *Firm wood graining applied to the table top.*

Below *MDF furniture can be made to look special with painting effects.*

FINDING INSPIRATION

It is fun to plan out a panelled room and introducing a variety of paint textures and techniques within the panels adds further dimensions to the decoration.

Walking around historic buildings and some of the older museums can stimulate ideas. The Victoria and Albert Museum in London was completely boarded up during World War II, the ceilings lowered and box-like corridors built. These protective measures remained in many beautiful buildings for years after and the interior design of the 1960s reflected this influence. In recent decades, however, these decorative areas have been uncovered to reveal the treats, treasures and delights hidden beneath. Ceilings may be painted in off white but they are divided into rounds, squares and oval decorated panelling, with wonderful detail.

Even in the smallest of rooms you too can paint a small alcove arch. If you place panels within small rooms over a piece of furniture the height of the room is naturally enhanced.

WOOD GRAINING

Wood graining is deceptively simple to do; it can be achieved with only an inexpensive plastic wood-graining roller. Here I have used wood graining directly on a white wall and over the top of an MDF (medium density fibreboard) table-top base coated with two layers of white. A very defined grain is achieved by pressing the roller firmly against the paint. More diffused wood graining with background texture is achieved by applying less pressure to a rubber wood-grainer. If you want a soft, worn look, just spray the finished damp wood graining with a mist spray and watch the ageing effect take place before your eyes.

Wood graining

I have painted all the furniture, wall panels and dado rail in this
sitting room in the same colour to give an airy, open feel. After
finishing the wall panel I decided to paint the surface of the table
in matching wood graining.

MATERIALS

Acrylic paint in your chosen colour

•

Spirit level

•

Tape measure or metal rule

•

Pair of compasses

•

Shallow container for paint

•

Paintbrush

•

Wood-graining roller

•

Art brush

1 Measure out the outside lines of the panel.
Use a spirit level to obtain accurate verticals
and for the top and bottom horizontals to the
depth required. Then mark in the width of the
panel frame.

2 Using a pair of compasses, mark out the corner
indentation. A variety of corner details is possible;
you might wish to repeat a detail from an ornate
mirror surround, for instance, or a curve within a
piece of furniture in your room.

82

MDF FURNITURE

Inexpensive furniture is readily available. All the furniture within this room is made from MDF and it can be bought in wonderful classic shapes that reproduce the styles of the past. Its surface is ideal for painting, so you can incorporate it into your individual colour scheme.

Often MDF furniture is exceptionally practical; for instance, the small table I have decorated with flowers has a drawer, so doubles as a desk. The bookcases on page 90 have deep drawers and shelves and as they are only MDF I have since drilled a hole through the back to take a dangling telephone cord and the wiring for a small lamp that crept onto the top shelf, without destroying a valuable piece of furniture.

MISTAKES

Do remember that if you are not happy with any of the effects that are appearing in your paint, be it wood graining over a wall or pretty flowers on furniture, you can just wipe the effect off if you keep a damp cloth to hand. I try most of my new techniques on good quality paper for acrylics and although it is not like a wall surface you can begin to get a feel for the paint.

Above *A quiet corner achieved by varying paint effects.*

Right *Detail of table leg design.*

Opposite *Positive wood graining on the table top is created by dragging the wood grainer firmly, removing more paint. Lighter, more diffused wood graining on the panel is achieved with a lighter dragging motion.*

Painting flowers on the table legs

To counter-balance the textured effect of the wood graining, flower motifs lighten and enliven the table. Part of the joy of decorating your own furniture is to choose what to place and where, by using only small parts of the templates if you wish.

MATERIALS

Template at back of book

•

Tracing paper

•

Pencil

•

Acrylic paint in three tones

•

Art brush

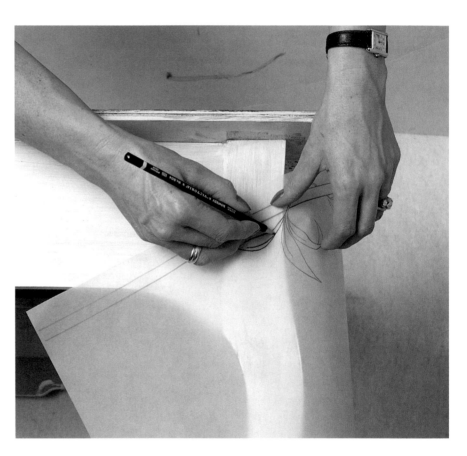

1 Trace the template. Hold elements of the design over the selected areas of furniture and even trace them on; you can rub out pencil marks if you are not happy with what you have chosen. Bend the design over the corners of the legs using elements of the leaves on one side and the stalk on the other as if the spray was actually growing.

2 To steady my hand while painting I rest my wrist on the table top; my little finger is also extended, touching the table leg and acting as an additional balance in an awkward situation. Paint in the whole flower and leaves in the lightest tone of purple. Follow the flow of each petal and your brush will give you all the textural movement required.

3 Each tracing template has shading detail drawn on it. Attach the template further up the table leg so that you can directly refer to it for help with shading. Make the purple a tone darker and touch the paint in on the design. Follow the guidelines on the template for directions of the brush strokes.

4 Again referring to the template, add even darker tone and give the final touch to the design. If you feel you have been over-zealous, have a slightly damp cloth to hand and gently dab it over any dense areas. Gentle patting is better than a wipe, which could remove too much paint. When the paint is dry rub out any pencil marks that show. Finally, varnish the piece to protect your work.

EXTENDING THE DESIGN

I have combined muted colours with chinoiserie-inspired designs in this room, which reflects my busy life yet conveys a sense of calm. I must also admit that this room has a dado rail on one wall and painted panels and a fireplace on the other. To be consistent I should have decorated the whole room following the same theme, but I just used elements that I liked in the same colour base, and the effect works well for me.

DADO RAIL

The wall beneath the dado rail has been painted with a gently dragged technique and the rail itself,

painted to look like bamboo, is decorated with tumbling flowers. This design gives me great pleasure and I know I shall reuse the theme in subsequent rooms in varying ways. I used the same design as for the bookcases on page 90, but adapted it slightly to give a softer effect.

There are no rules when using designs; decorating is entirely a matter of personal choice. Generally, though, it is sensible to reduce designs for small areas and to enlarge them for large areas. Use the templates at the back of the book to suit your own setting, perhaps choosing just one bud rather than a whole bouquet, or breaking the design at intervals for clear space.

Above *Enlarging elements of the template at the back of the book gives an effective design to enhance a dividing dado line.*

Left *Natural harmony is created within the room by using the same colours for the different effects.*

Right *The complete design is used on both sides of the bookcases.*

Opposite *The lamp table is practical and can be moved around the room. Its circular design shows to good effect wherever the table is placed.*

Below *Elements of the bamboo design are used to enclose an area of soft dragging.*

Bottom *The design is adapted for the small space between the handles of the drawer.*

BOOKCASES

Painting furniture allows great expression of individuality. I thoroughly enjoyed decorating these pieces; with a dustsheet spread over the floor and the furniture on its side in the most convenient position for painting, I snuggled down with some music to listen to for hours of creative inspiration and pleasure.

When deciding on projects make sure you give yourself enough time. The base coats have to be completed at the same time, but painting motifs can be done at your leisure, leaving weeks in between. There is no need to rush to finish the bookcases, for example.

Planning out areas and how to use the tracings from the template gives you a unique chance to decide on the decorative areas for your furniture. I decided to paint the drawer of the table with a single flower blossom, but have given the drawers of the bookcases a stylized geometric design reflecting the wood panelling on the walls. However, I have used the full bamboo and flower design on the sides of the bookcases.

LAMP TABLE

The little lamp table lent itself to a circular design. To achieve this I first drew a circle of the same diameter as the table with a pair of compasses. Then I simply traced the elements of the design within the circle.

Painting a bamboo effect

The full geometric bamboo design is used in steps that mount the
sides of the bookcases, but the pattern can be adapted back to the
simplest dip in a line when combined with flowers for the dado rail.
Choose a design that suits your particular purpose.

MATERIALS

Template at back of book

•

Acrylic paint in your chosen colour

•

Tracing paper

•

Pencil

•

Straightedge or ruler

•

Art brush

•

Felt-tip pen

•

Large flat art brush

1 Trace the template at the back of the book.
Then go over the lines on one side of the template
in pencil, fix the template into position with
masking tape to avoid movement and transfer back
the design onto your piece of furniture. Use a
ruler on straight lines; if your guideline is not
straight your paint line will suffer.

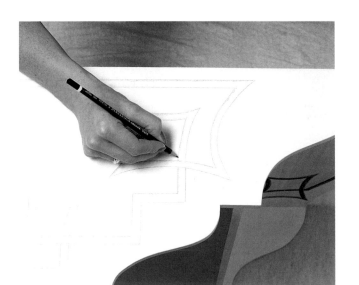

2 Remove the tracing and go over any faint lines in
pencil. Trace out all the elements of the design if it
will help you as the second coat of shading paint
will cover the pencil markings. Otherwise trace
out the outlines and when painting keep the
template to hand so that you can copy additional
detail or the direction of the brush strokes.

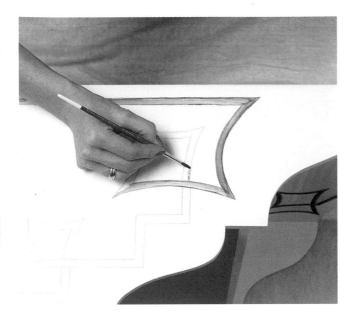

3 Paint all the lightest purple tone in. Do not be concerned if the paint is not completely even; it is very difficult to keep it so. Concentrate on each line and get that as even as you can.

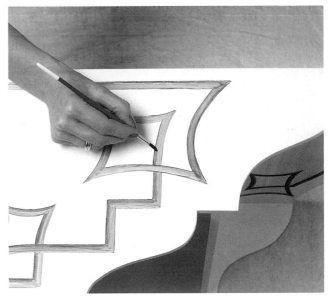

5 Make the purple paint used in the first coat slightly darker with a touch of black paint, then apply a line of colour on the shaded side. Note in all these painting progressions that my wrist is firmly on the furniture steadying my hand.

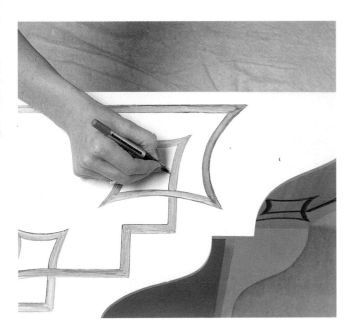

4 Draw over with a felt tip along the side of the template that is most shaded. This little cheating tip is most effective; the felt tip will mask any slight wiggles of the brush and when used against the ruler on the straight lines, give a very neat edge.

6 Dilute the acrylic paint to ink consistency. Then shake it well and check the tone over white paper. With a wider brush stroke the paint over the white to create a dragged effect. On the long side slide your wrist down the edge of the furniture as you drag the brush along. Varnish the furniture several times for protection.

Suppliers

Daler-Rowney Fine Art and Graphics Materials

Daler-Rowney Ltd, P. O. Box 10,
Bracknell, Berks RG12 8ST.
Tel 01344 424621. Fax 01344 486511.

Working with these exceptionally high quality products always gives the best results. System 3 acrylic paints are versatile and easy to use, the brushes hard wearing and subtle. I use many Daler-Rowney products, from the finest of brushes to a wide choice of papers and paints. A full 156-page catalogue available from the company demonstrates the diversity of the products and gives constructive information on using materials.

Dulux (ICI Paints)

Wexham Road, Slough, Berkshire SL2 5DS.

Dulux has recently developed ten Special Effects Paints in a subtle range of colours. Special Effects Paints are pre-mixed and ready to go. All you do is choose your colour and combined with the right brush or tools the effect is easy to achieve. The paints are water soluble and odourless. Dulux has the widest selection of all paints with excellent colour cards to help you choose your individual colour theme within your home. Dulux is available from most hardware shops and many other points of distribution.

Scumble Goosie

Lewiston Mill, Brimscombe, Stroud,
Gloucestershire GL5 2TB.
Tel/Fax 01453 731305.

Scumble Goosie run by Nicola and Jon Madeley make fine MDF and wood furniture. All the designs are excellent, from tables and bookcases, to wall cupboards and chests of drawers, and smaller lamps and fire screens. An excellent catalogue is available and the company distributes throughout Europe.

Jali Shelves

Apsley House, Chartham, Canterbury,
Kent CT4 7HT.
Tel 01227 831710. Fax 01227 831950.

Jali make decorative trims for shelving, pelmets, brackets and self-assembly kits. A well-presented catalogue is available and the mail order service very prompt.

Stanley Tools

Wellington Road, Leeds LS12 1DU.
Tel 0113 263 0221. Fax 0113 231 0194.

Stanley Tools have developed the full range of specialist paint equipment and brushes for sponging, wood graining and stippling – everything needed for successful paint effects – not to mention the multitude of tools the company produces for amateur and professional alike. Stanley Tools are distributed throughout the UK and the specialist paints equipment can be found on sale at outlets with Dulux paint.

The Decorative Arts Company Ltd

5a Royal Crescent, London W11 4SI.
Tel 0171 371 4303. Fax 0171 602 9189.

The Decorative Arts Company supplies many and varied small objects from trays to clocks, shelves to boxes, to name but a few. Decorative Arts also runs courses and has a mail order catalogue and distributes throughout Europe.

Stevenson Brothers

The Workshop, Ashford Road, Bethersden,
Ashford, Kent TN26 3AP.
Tel 01233 820363. Fax 01233 820580.

Stevenson Brothers not only make the most beautiful rocking horse, but restore old friends. Stevenson Brothers gave new life to the horse on page 40, giving me advice on specialist paint techniques for the best finish. My daughter's horse will now return to them to be expertly tacked up and have mane and tail properly attached. A full colour brochure is available with information on restoration of old horses throughout the UK.

Manuel Canovas

2 North Terrace, London SW3 2BA.
Tel 0171 225 2298. Fax 0171 823 7848.

Beautifully designed fabrics.

Design templates

The following templates are ready for you to tear out or trace.
You can photocopy them to enlarge or reduce them or change them
to suit a particular project. See page 96 for how to do so.

Adapting tracing templates

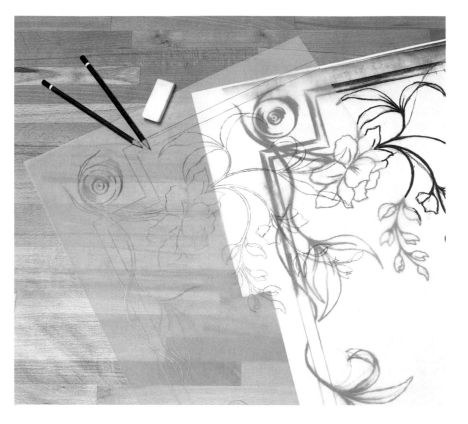

ENLARGING A DESIGN

The templates at the back of the book can be used in any way you want. Enlarge them on a photocopier. If you wish to enlarge them to an A3 size you can save yourself time by placing an A3 piece of tracing paper in the photocopier's paper tray and avoid having to trace off normal paper copies.

When you enlarge a design by photocopying, several sections of the motif will appear on differing sheets. Assemble them as you would a jigsaw puzzle, tape them into position and place a large tracing paper sheet over the top and trace off in pencil.

CHANGING THE SHAPE OF THE TEMPLATE

To compile a totally different design, into a circular motif from a square one, for instance, draw a circle using a pair of compasses. Then place elements of the design over the template, and trace the chosen parts so that they curve around the new tracing. Remember that you can flip over your tracing, have it going back, up, down or sideways – you are creating something new. When you flip a design over, however, make sure that you have pencil lines on both sides when you trace through onto furniture.

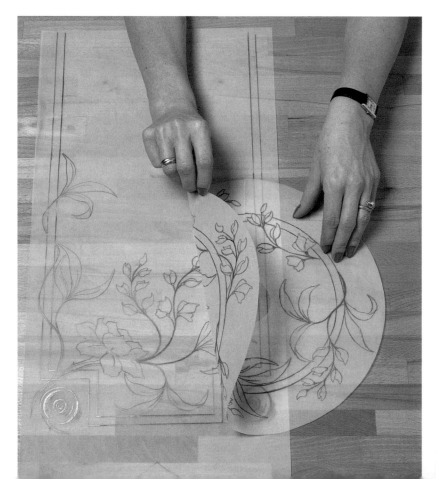

DOTS AND SPRIGS

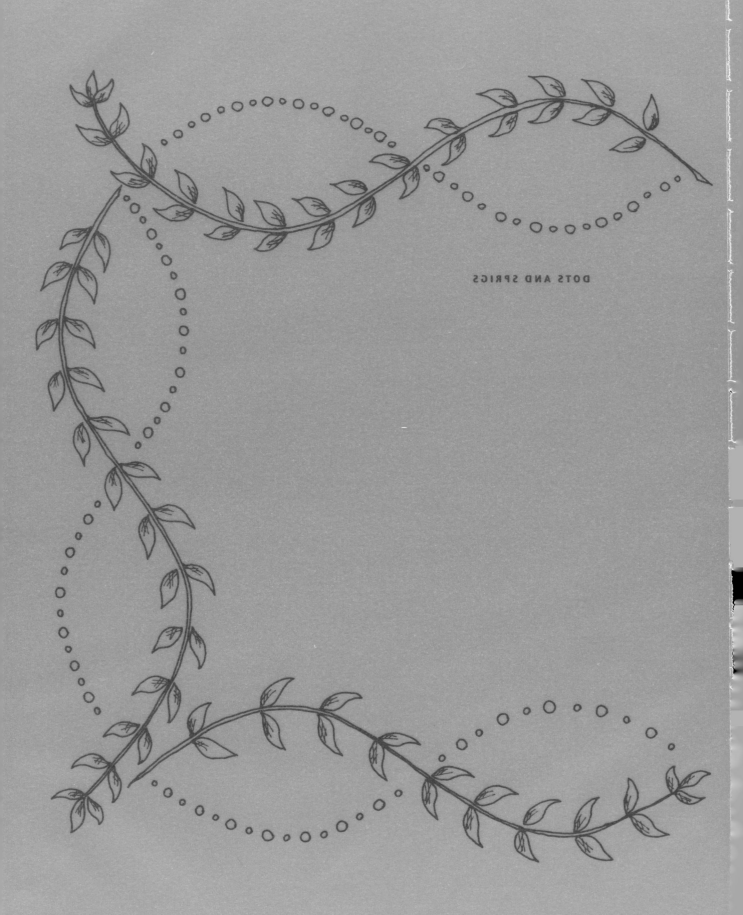

DOTS AND SPRIGS

IVY

DAISIES

1234567890

IVY

DAISIES

1234567890

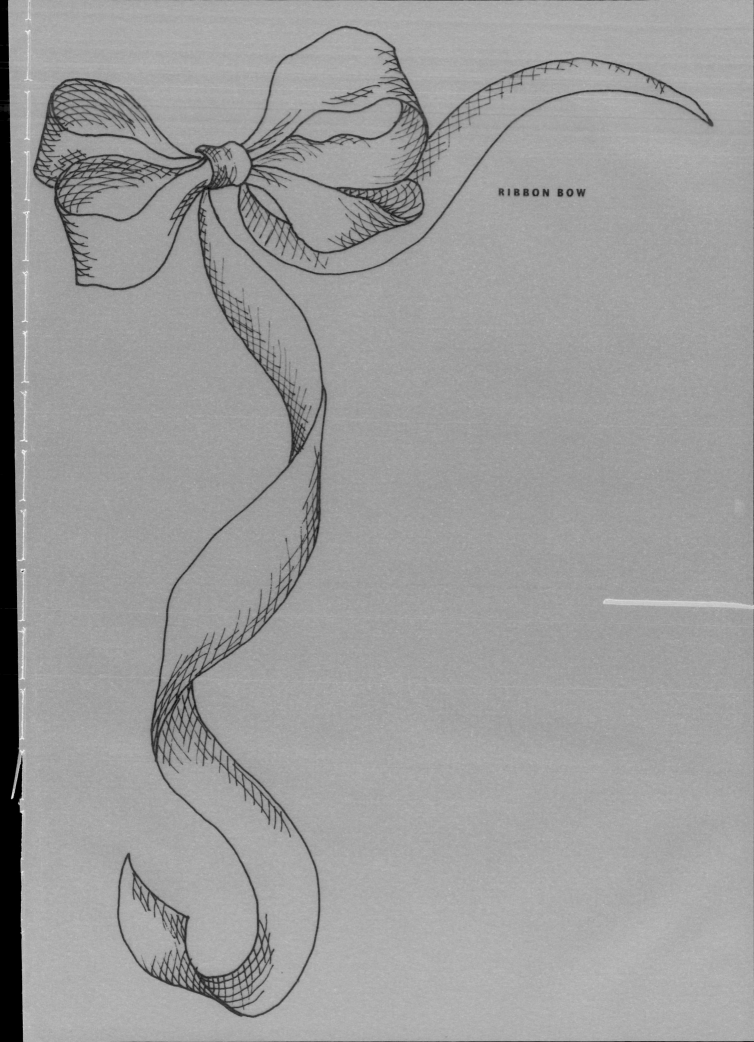

RIBBON BOW

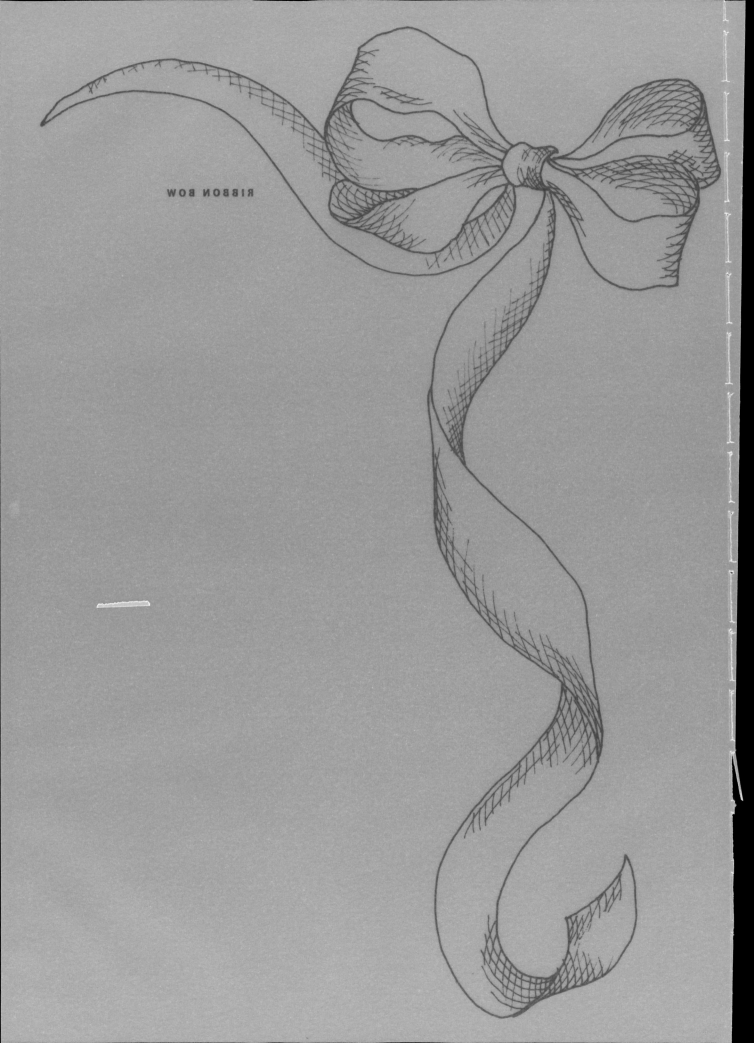

RIBBON BOW

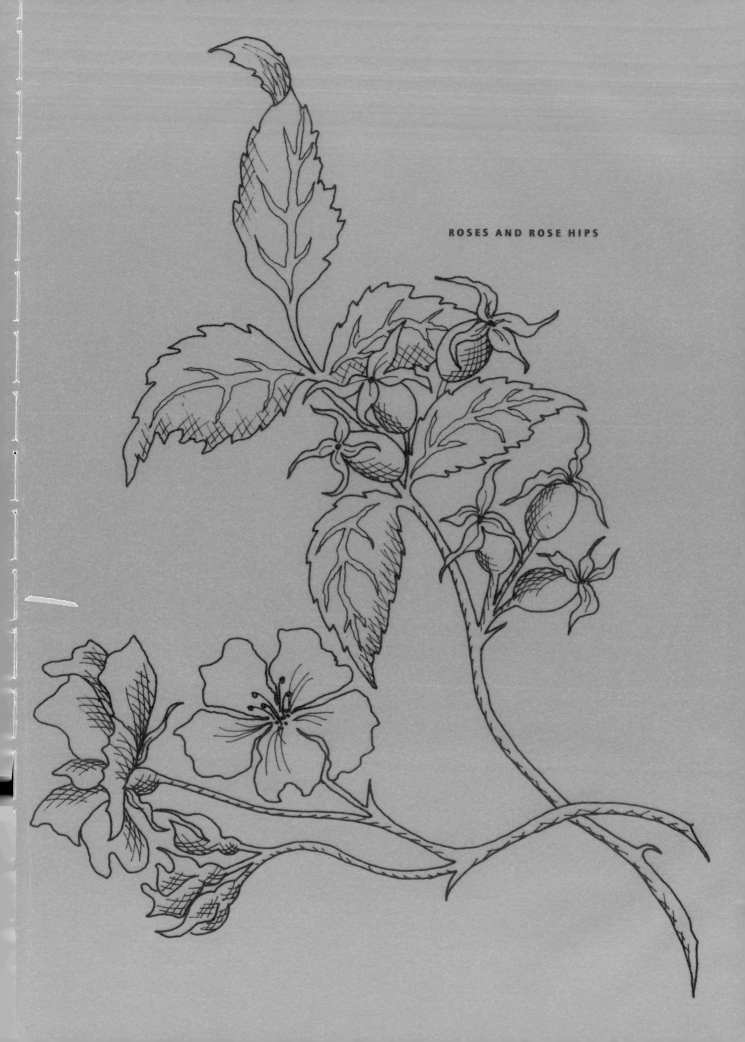

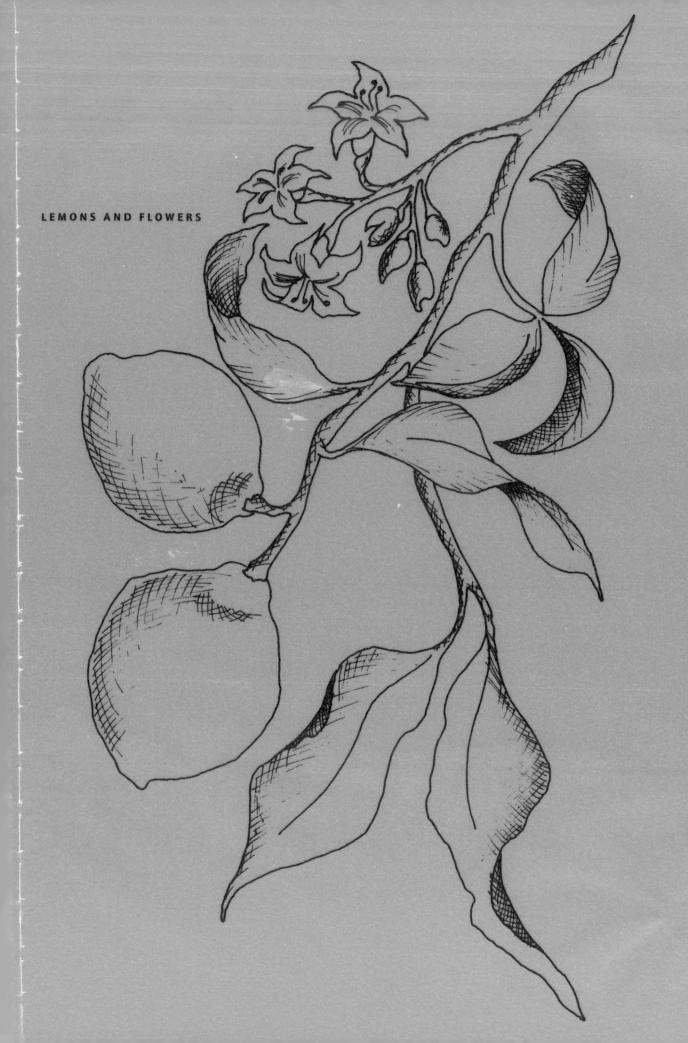

LEMONS AND FLOWERS

LEMONS

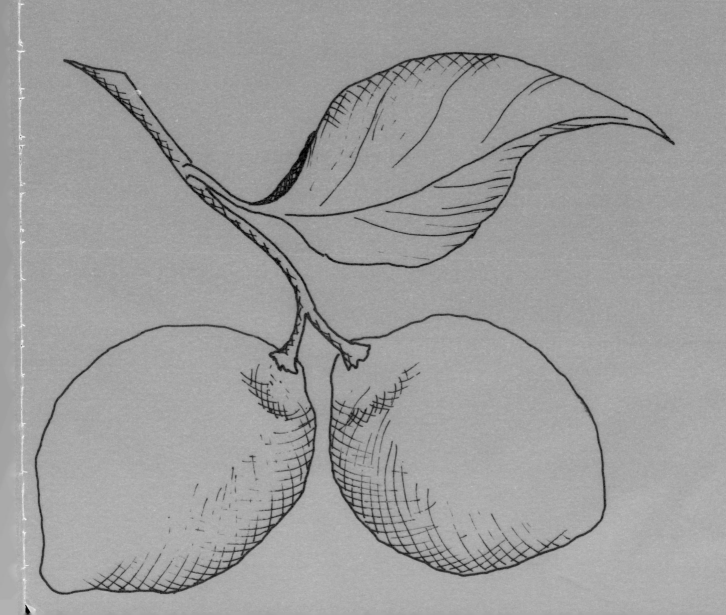

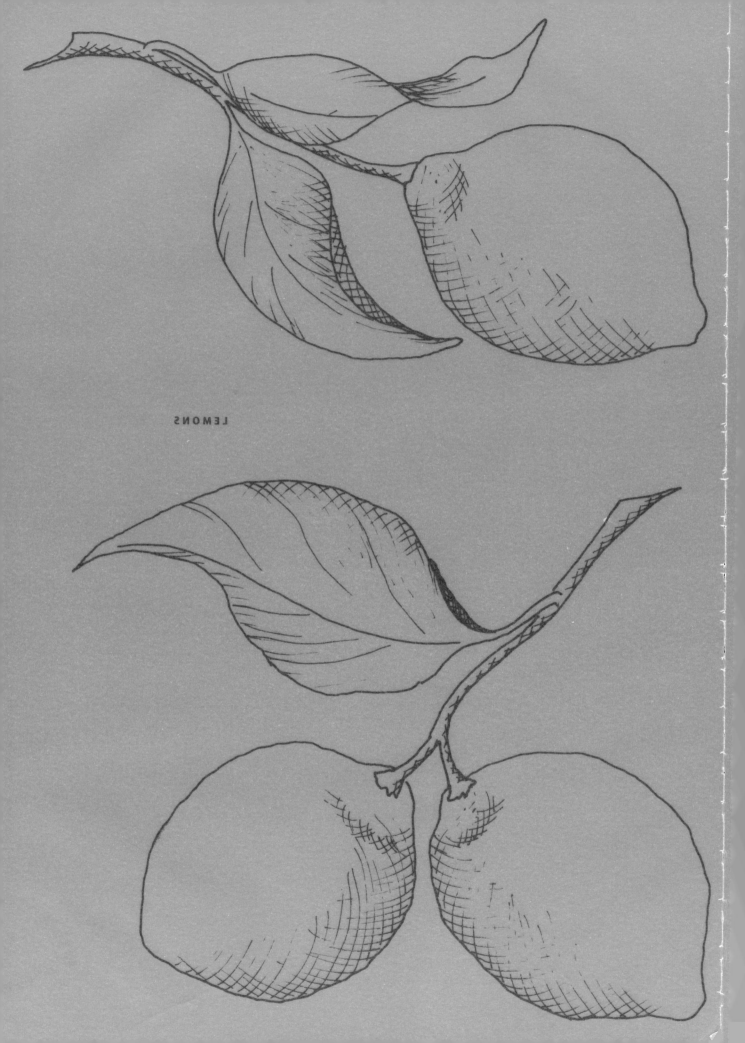

LEMONS

FLOWER SPRAY AND BAMBOO PANEL

FLOWER SPRAY AND BAMBOO PANEL

BAMBOO PANEL

BAMBOO PANEL